Wild Dogs

Wolves, Coyotes and Foxes

Written by Deborah Hodge

Illustrated by Pat Stephens

KIDS CAN PRESS
WILDLIFE SERIES

Kids Can Press Ltd.,
Toronto

For my brothers, Chris and Pete, and in memory of my sister, Mala - DH
To Rick and Tiger, and in memory of Kiri - PS

I would like to acknowledge with thanks the review of my manuscript by John P. Elliot, Regional Wildlife Biologist, British Columbia Ministry of Environment, Lands and Parks.

I would also like to thank the hardworking people at Kids Can Press — in particular, my editor, Valerie Wyatt, for her continuing patience and tact, and my publishers, Valerie Hussey and Ricky Englander, for their vision and drive.

Thanks are also due to my own "wild dog," Sally, who gave me daily opportunities to observe canine habits and behaviour.

Kids Can Press Ltd. acknowledges with appreciation the assistance of the Canada Council and the Ontario Arts Council in the production of this book.

Cataloguing in Publication Data

Hodge, Deborah
  Wild dogs : wolves, coyotes and foxes
(Kids Can Press wildlife series)
Includes index.
ISBN 1-55074-360-0

1. Wild dogs — Juvenile literature. 2. Foxes — Juvenile literature. 3. Wolves — Juvenile literature. 4. Coyotes — Juvenile literature.
I. Stephens, Pat. II. Title. III. Series.

QL737.C22H63   1996   j599.74'442
C96-931293-8

Text copyright © 1997 by Deborah Hodge
Illustrations copyright © 1997 by Pat Stephens

Kids Can Press Ltd.
29 Birch Avenue
Toronto, Ontario, Canada
M4V 1E2

Edited by Valerie Wyatt
Designed by Marie Bartholomew
Printed in Hong Kong by Wing King Tong
Company Ltd.

97 0 9 8 7 6 5 4 3 2 1

Contents

Wild dogs   4

Kinds of wild dogs   6

Where wild dogs live   8

How wild dogs live   10

Wild dog food   12

Wild dog bodies   14

How wild dogs move   16

Wild dog homes   18

How wild dogs are born   20

How wild dogs grow and learn   22

How wild dogs protect themselves   24

Wild dogs and people   26

Wild dogs of the world   28

Wild dog signs   30

Words to know   31

Index   32

Wild dogs

Coyotes, wolves and foxes are all wild dogs. They have strong bodies, long legs and a keen sense of smell. Wild dogs are swift runners and skilled hunters.

Wild dogs are mammals. Mammals have fur to keep them warm and lungs for breathing. They are warm-blooded. Their body temperature stays about the same, even when the temperature around them changes.

Mammal babies are born live. They drink their mother's milk. These young foxes are hungry!

Pet dogs are related to wild dogs. They are alike in many ways.

These wolves are howling. People rarely see wild dogs, but they sometimes hear their lonesome cries.

Kinds of wild dogs

There are three main kinds of wild dogs in North America: coyotes, foxes and wolves.

Coyotes are grey or brown. An adult can weigh from 9 to 18 kg (20 to 40 pounds) – about the same as a medium-sized dog. As with other wild dogs, the females are usually smaller than the males.

Coyote

Red fox

Swift fox

Grey fox

Arctic fox

There are four kinds of foxes in North America. Red foxes are the most common. A red fox can be red, brown, black or silver. Most adult males weigh about 5.5 kg (12 pounds).

Most wolves are grey wolves. The colour of a grey wolf's fur depends on where it lives. In the Arctic the fur is white; in the forest it is grey or black. An adult grey wolf is about the size of a big German shepherd. It can weigh from 26 to 59 kg (57 to 130 pounds). There are also a few red wolves in North America.

Red wolf

Grey wolf

Where wild dogs live

Every wild dog needs a habitat – a place where it can get the food, water, shelter and space it needs to stay alive.

Wolves live in wild areas in North America, Europe and Asia. They make their homes in forests, prairies and the Arctic tundra. Wolves try to stay away from people and close to the animals they hunt.

Coyotes and foxes can live almost anywhere – in forests, fields, mountains, prairies or deserts. Coyotes are found only in North America, but foxes live in many parts of the world.

Arctic foxes live in cold, northern areas. In the summer, when the snow is gone, their fur turns brown.

Foxes often hide in tall grass to hunt mice and other small animals.

How wild dogs live

Some wild dogs live alone. Others live in close family groups called packs.

Wolves belong to packs of 2 to 20 wolves. The pack travels and hunts together. Pack members protect and care for one another. Coyotes often live in pairs or small packs. Foxes live alone unless they are caring for baby foxes.

Wolves use body signals to show who the leader is. The alpha wolf holds its head and tail high. The other wolf crouches low.

In a pack, the
alpha wolves
always eat first.

Every wolf pack has an alpha male and alpha female. They
are the strongest and wisest wolves. They lead the pack.

Wild dog food

Wild dogs are meat eaters. They hunt and kill other animals – their prey.

Wolves hunt large hoofed animals such as moose, deer, elk and caribou. A pack hunts together, chasing and circling its prey.

Coyotes and foxes hunt mice, ground squirrels and rabbits. They also feed on insects, frogs, fish, birds, eggs, wild fruit and berries. Coyotes may eat deer and the remains of dead animals.

This coyote is hunting a tasty fish.

A fox uses its nose to find prey, even under the snow.

Wild dog bodies

A wild dog's body is built for hunting and chasing.

Ears
Sharp ears can hear prey moving in the grass or under the snow.

Nose
A keen sense of smell helps the wild dog sniff out prey and tell where other wild dogs have been.

Tongue
Running makes the wild dog hot. It cools down by panting.

Jaws and teeth
Powerful jaws grab the prey. Pointy fangs make a killing bite. Razor-sharp teeth slice off pieces of meat, which are swallowed whole.

Muscles
Strong muscles help a wild dog catch and kill its prey. A powerful neck helps the dog pull its prey to the ground.

Fur

A wild dog has two kinds of fur. Soft underfur keeps it warm in winter. Long guard hair protects the wild dog from rain and snow. The colour helps it blend in with its surroundings.

Bones

A wild dog's skeleton is built for running. Its bones are light but sturdy.

Tail

The position of the tail sends signals to other wild dogs. Scent glands at the base of the tail let a wild dog mark off its home area.

Legs and toes

Long, slender legs help a wild dog run fast and far without tiring. The dog runs swiftly on its toes. Toe pads absorb the shock of running.

How wild dogs move

Wild dogs are graceful runners. They run almost silently, taking big strides. Wild dogs can trot for hours and travel a long way without tiring. When they are chasing prey, wild dogs run very fast. They are also good swimmers.

A fox hunts like a cat. It crouches low, then pounces!

Wolves and coyotes can leap great distances – up to 4.5 m (15 feet) in one jump.

At top speed, a coyote travels faster than a car on a city street – up to 60 km/h (40 miles per hour).

Wild dog homes

For most of the year, wild dogs don't have homes. Instead, they have resting spots close to their hunting areas.

When a female wild dog is ready to have babies, she finds an unused den or digs a new one. Most dens are dug into a hillside, near water. The entrance is often hidden by bushes, rocks or a fallen log.

This wolf den makes a cosy home for the new pups. There are several tunnels out, so the mother and pups can escape if danger threatens.

WILD DOG FACT

A wild dog often digs more than one den.

Wild dogs often borrow dens made by other animals. This fox is cleaning out an old badger den.

Some wild dogs, such as this coyote, use the same den year after year.

How wild dogs are born

In the spring, a wild dog crawls into her den and gives birth. She may have up to 13 pups, but smaller litters of 4 to 6 pups are common.

The newborn pups are tiny, blind and deaf. The mother washes them with her tongue. She guides them to her nipples so they can feed on her rich milk.

This mother coyote senses danger, so she moves her pups to a new den.

WILD DOG FACT

Father wild dogs protect their new families by keeping watch outside the den.

Newborn fox pups nestle close to their mother. Her furry body keeps them warm.

How wild dogs grow and learn

The pups take their first wobbly steps inside the den. By four weeks, they begin to play at the den's entrance. Soon they spend much of their time outdoors.

Very young pups eat meat that their parents bring them. At two months of age, they are ready to learn to hunt. The adults teach the pups how to catch prey and protect themselves.

By fall, young foxes begin to live alone. Coyote families may split up or stay together, depending on the food supply. Young wolves stay with their pack for one or more years.

Young pups learn to nip at an adult's mouth. This signals the adult to bring up food from its stomach for the pup to eat.

Pups like to play. These coyote pups wrestle and pounce on one another. Playing builds muscles and teaches hunting skills.

How wild dogs protect themselves

Wolves have no real enemies except for bears and other wolf packs. They would rather flee than fight.

Foxes fear coyotes, wolves, black bears, bobcats, lynx and cougars. They protect themselves by running away or hiding in thick bushes or dens.

A coyote's enemies are black bears, cougars and wolves. A coyote tries to run from its enemies. If cornered, a coyote will fight.

Every wolf pack has its home area where it lives and hunts. Pack members howl to let other wolves know the area is taken. They also spray urine along the edges of the home area. This scent signal tells other wolves to stay away.

Wild dogs and people

Years ago, people feared wolves. Many wolves were hunted and killed, so there are far fewer wolves today. Wolves try to stay away from people. But as wild areas shrink, there is less space for wolves to roam and raise their young.

Coyotes and foxes may live near people. Many settle around farms or ranches and even in cities. With wolves gone from these areas, there is less danger and more food for the smaller wild dogs. So the numbers of foxes and coyotes keep growing.

Wild dogs can live for up to 12 years, but most die in their first year of life.

All wild dogs need clean water, lots of food and enough space to live and grow.

27

Wild dogs of the world

There are 35 species of wild dogs in the world. Here are some of them.

Maned wolf
South America

Bush dog
South America

Fennec fox
Africa

**African hunting dog
(or hyena)**
Africa

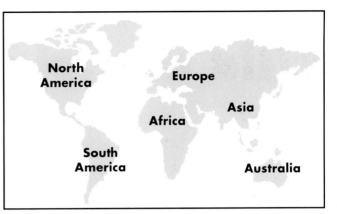

Dingo
Australia

Raccoon dog
Europe and Asia

Golden jackal
Africa and Asia

Wild dog signs

Tracks

Coyote and wolf tracks look like the footprints of a dog. Fox tracks look more like cat prints. These prints are life-size. How do they compare with the paw prints of your cat or dog?

Grey wolf

Red fox

Coyote

Scat

Scat is the name for wild dog droppings or body waste. Scat sometimes has pieces of feathers, fur or bones in it. It can tell you what the wild dog was eating. Can you guess what this fox ate?

Answer: A bird.

30

Words to know

alpha female: the female leader in a wolf pack

alpha male: the male leader in a wolf pack

den: an underground home for a mother wild dog and her pups

habitat: the place where an animal naturally lives and grows

mammal: a warm-blooded animal with hair covering, whose babies are born live and fed mother's milk

pack: a family group of wild dogs that live and hunt together

prey: an animal that is hunted for food

pup: a young wild dog

scat: wild dog droppings or body waste

tundra: large, flat, treeless areas in the Arctic

warm-blooded: having a warm body temperature, even when it is cold outside

Index

African hunting dogs, 28
age, 22, 27
alpha wolves, 10, 11, 31
Arctic foxes, 6, 8

baby wild dogs. *See* pups
birth, 4, 20, 21
body, 4, 10, 14, 15, 31
   bones, 15
   ears, 14
   fur, 4, 7, 8, 15, 21
   head, 10
   jaws, 14
   legs, 4, 15
   mouth, 14, 22
   muscles, 14, 23
   neck, 14
   nose, 14
   stomach, 22
   tail, 10, 15
   teeth, 14
   temperature, 4, 14, 21, 31
   toes, 15
   tongue, 14
bush dogs, 28

colouring, 6, 7, 8, 15
coyotes, 4, 6, 8, 9, 10,
   12, 16, 17, 19, 20,
   22, 23, 24, 26, 30

dens, 18, 19, 20, 21, 22,
   24, 31
dingoes, 29
dogs, pet, 5

enemies, 24. *See also*
   protection

families, 10, 21, 22, 31
fennec foxes, 28
food, 4, 8, 9, 11, 12, 13,
   14, 20, 22, 26
foxes, 4, 6, 8, 9, 10, 12, 13,
   16, 19, 21, 22, 24, 26
fur, 4, 7, 8, 15, 21

golden jackals, 29
grey foxes, 6
grey wolves, 7, 30
growing up, 22, 23, 27

habitats, 8, 31
home areas, 15, 25
homes. *See* dens
howling, 5, 25
hunting, 4, 8, 9, 10, 12, 14,
   16, 18, 22, 23, 25, 31
hyenas, 28

jackals, 29
jumping, 16

learning, 22, 23
litter size, 20

mammals, 4, 31
maned wolves, 28
mother's milk, 4, 20, 31

packs, 10, 11, 12, 22,
   24, 25, 31

people, 8, 26
playing, 22, 23
prey, 9, 12, 13, 14, 16,
   22, 31
protection, 10, 15, 18,
   20, 21, 22, 24, 25
pups, 4, 10, 18, 20, 21,
   22, 23, 31

raccoon dogs, 29
red foxes, 6, 30
red wolves, 7
running, 4, 15, 16, 17, 24

scat, 30, 31
senses, 14, 20
signals, 10, 15, 22, 25
sizes, 6, 7
species, 6, 7, 28, 29
swift foxes, 6
swimming, 16

tracks, 30
tundra, 8, 31
types of wild dogs.
   See species

warm-blooded, 4, 31
weights, 6, 7
wolves, 4, 5, 6, 7, 8, 10,
   11, 12, 16, 18, 22,
   24, 26

young. *See* pups